Our World

Living and growing

Neil Morris

Thameside Press

US publication copyright © 2002 Thameside Press
International copyright reserved in all countries.
No part of this book may be reproduced in any form
without written permission from the publisher.

Distributed in the United States by
Smart Apple Media
1980 Lookout Drive
North Mankato, MN 56003

Text copyright © Neil Morris 2002

Printed in Hong Kong

ISBN 1-930643-80-2

Library of Congress Control Number 2002 141320

Series editor: Jean Coppendale
Designer: Peter Clayman
Artwork: Chris Forsey
Picture researchers: Terry Forshaw, Louise Daubeny, Jenny Barlow and Ashley Brent
Consultant: Bethan Currenti

Printed in Hong Kong

10 9 8 7 6 5 4 3 2 1

Picture acknowledgments:
(T) = Top, (B) = Bottom, (L) = Left, (R) = Right.
Animal Photography = AP, C = Corbis, CI = Chrysalis Images, CO = Collections DV = Digital Vision, E = Ecoscene, FLPA = Frank Lane Picture Agency, GM = Garden Matters, SPL = Science Photo Library.

Front Cover (main) & 8 (B) Doug Wilson/C; Title Page, 17 (B) & front cover (inset) CI; 4 (T) Robert Pickett, (B) Dr Yorgos Nikas/SPL; 5 Alissa Crandall/C; 6 Garry Watson/SPL; 7 DV; 8 (T) & back cover (L) DV; 9 Manfred Kage/SPL; 10 Sally Anne Thompson/AP; 11 & front cover (inset) Terry Andrewartha/FLPA; 12 & back cover (R) CI; 13 CI; 14 Warren Morgan/C; 15 Juergen Berger, Max Planck Institute/SPL; 16 & front cover (inset) CI; 17 (T) CI; 18 Quest/SPL; 19 CNRI/SPL; 20 Minden Pictures/FLPA; 21, front cover (inset) & 31 (R) Laura Dwight/C; 22 Debi Wager, Stock Pics/GM; 23 Jeremy Hoare/GM; 24 & 25 Graham Kitching/E; 26 (T) Andrew Brown/C, (B) & 31 (L) Tony Wharton, FLPA/C; 27 Paul Bryans/CO.

Contents

Living things	4
How babies grow	6
Growing up	8
Different rates and sizes	10
Food for growth	12
Getting better	14
Changing shape	16
Chemical messengers	18
Growing and learning	20
How plants grow	22
The growing season	24
Life cycle	26
Do it yourself	28
Glossary	30
Index	32

Living things

All things grow, getting bigger and heavier as time passes. This is because all the world's people, animals, and plants begin their lives as a single, tiny **cell**.

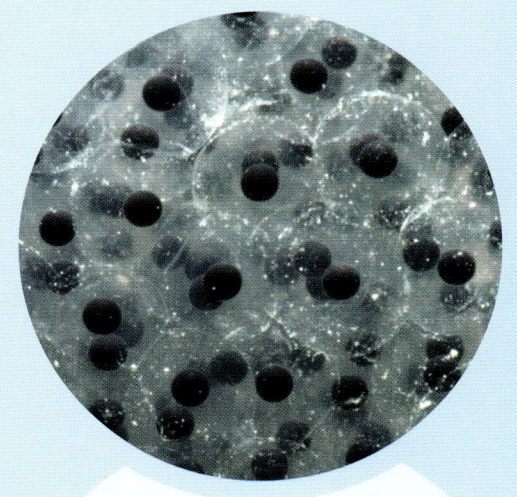

Frogs lay eggs in a sticky jelly that protects them as they grow.

We can see tiny cells through a microscope. This picture shows a human cell that has divided into eight.

Birds' cells first grow in an egg. An ostrich's eggs are the biggest in the world.

Cells let living things grow by **multiplying** themselves. The first cell **divides** to make two cells, which then divide to make four cells. And so it goes on until there are millions of cells.

How babies grow

Human babies also start life as a single cell, inside their mother's body. The cells go on multiplying and growing inside the mother. It takes about nine months for them to become a fully formed baby.

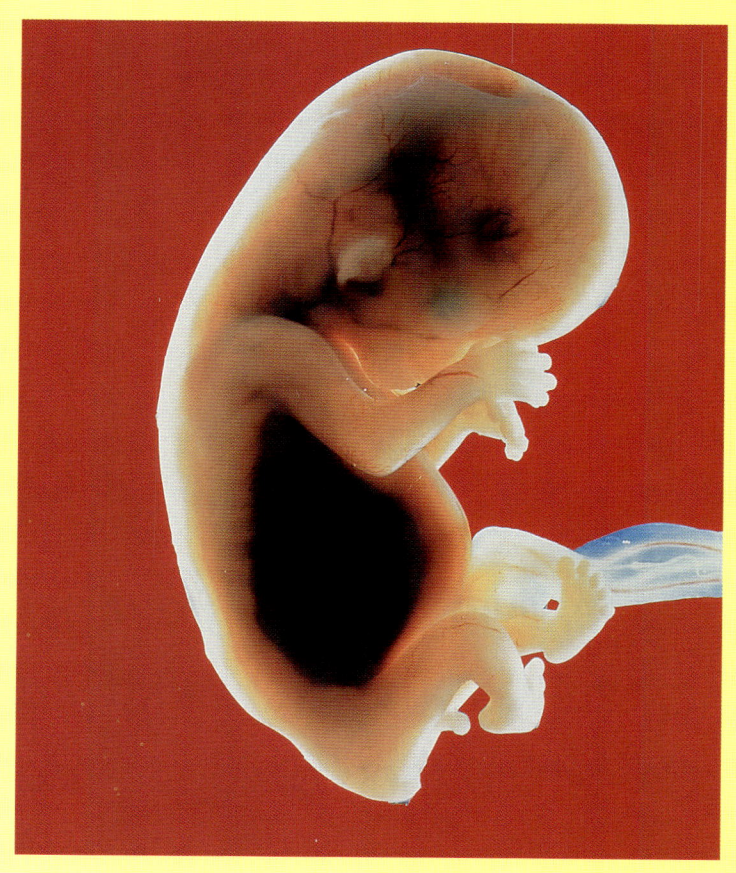

This picture shows a human baby developing inside its mother's body.

Babies soon learn how to move around by crawling.

After they are born, babies go on growing very fast. By the time children are two years old, they are about half as tall as they will be when they are fully grown adults.

Growing up

Children need a lot of love and care from their parents.

Young boys and girls have a lot of **energy**. Games are fun and good for growing bodies.

Once boys and girls are old enough to walk and talk, they go on growing at a slower pace. Children reach about three-quarters of their adult height by the age of nine.

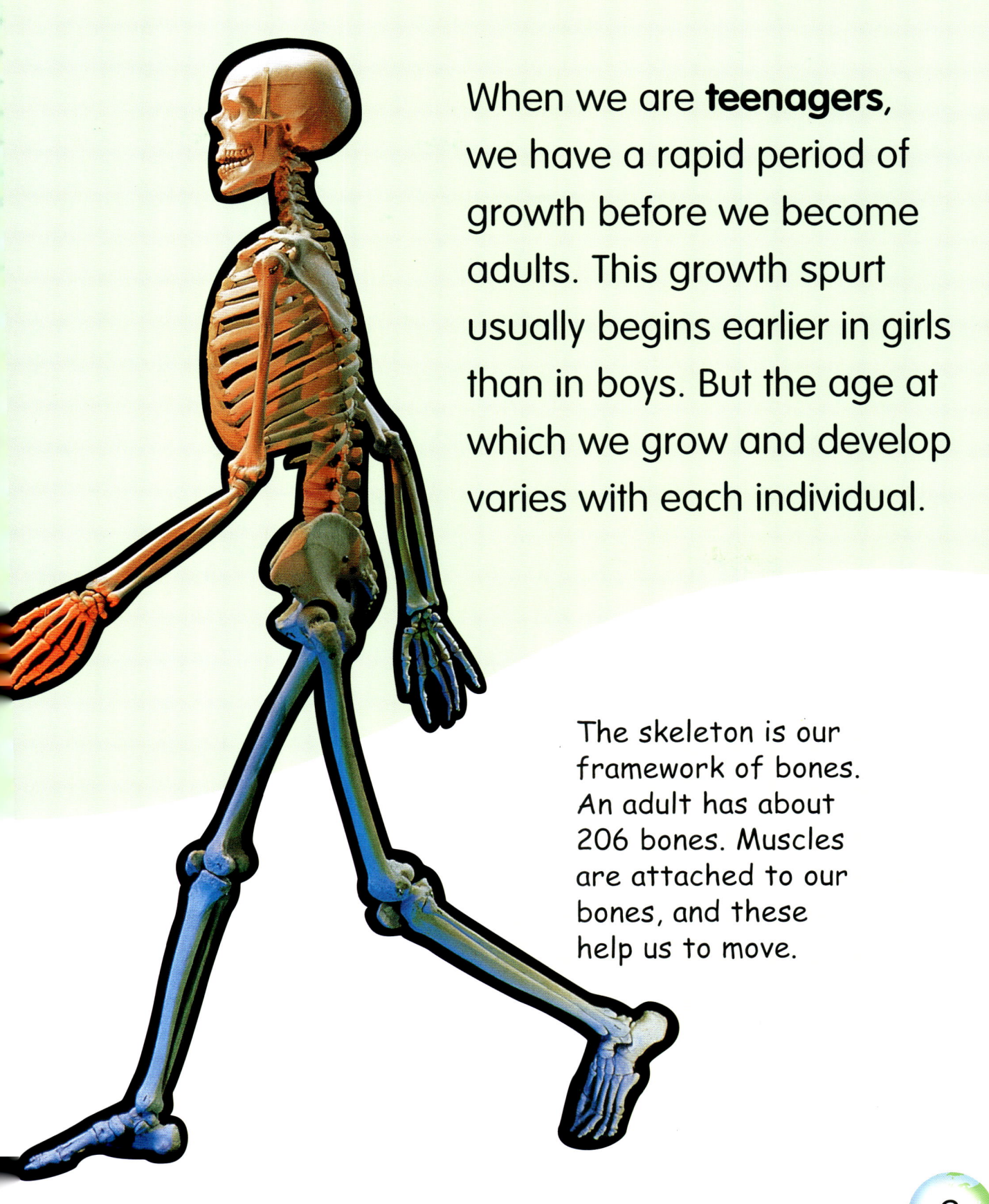

When we are **teenagers**, we have a rapid period of growth before we become adults. This growth spurt usually begins earlier in girls than in boys. But the age at which we grow and develop varies with each individual.

The skeleton is our framework of bones. An adult has about 206 bones. Muscles are attached to our bones, and these help us to move.

Different rates and sizes

Animals grow at different rates and end up being very different sizes. Land animals cannot simply keep on growing, because if they were too heavy, their bones would not be able to support their weight.

An adult guinea pig is about five times heavier than its baby. The youngster soon puts on weight.

In the same way, muscles would not have the power to move animals if they were too big and heavy. An adult elephant is about 40 times heavier than a baby elephant. But in many other animals, adults are not much bigger than their growing children.

A baby elephant looks tiny next to its mother.

Food for growth

All living things need energy to grow, and they get that energy from what they eat and drink. Some foods contain lots of **proteins**, which help us stay healthy and grow.

Sheep are plant eaters. But like humans, baby lambs begin life by drinking their mother's milk.

Lions, tigers, and other big cats are all meat eaters. The adults hunt for food.

Some animals, such as elephants, eat only plants. Others, such as lions, eat the meat of other animals. In this way, animals form a **food chain**, with large birds eating small animals, which eat insects, which eat plants, and so on.

Getting better

As humans and animals grow, they sometimes become ill or hurt themselves. Their bodies have special ways of helping with these problems, and they may grow new cells to heal wounds.

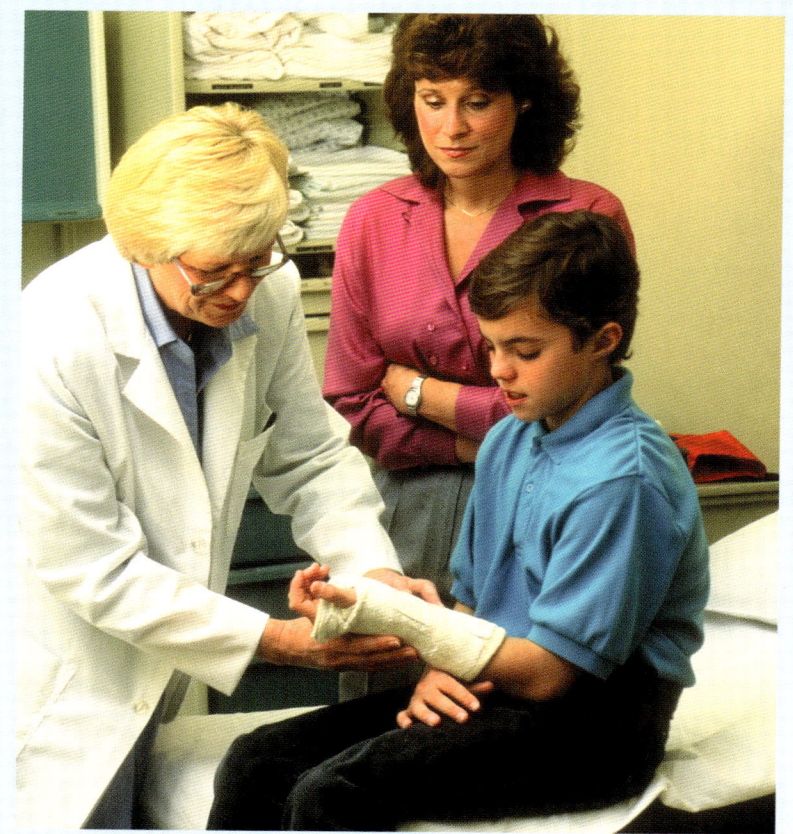

If we break one of our bones, plaster helps to keep it still. The bone mends itself by growing together again.

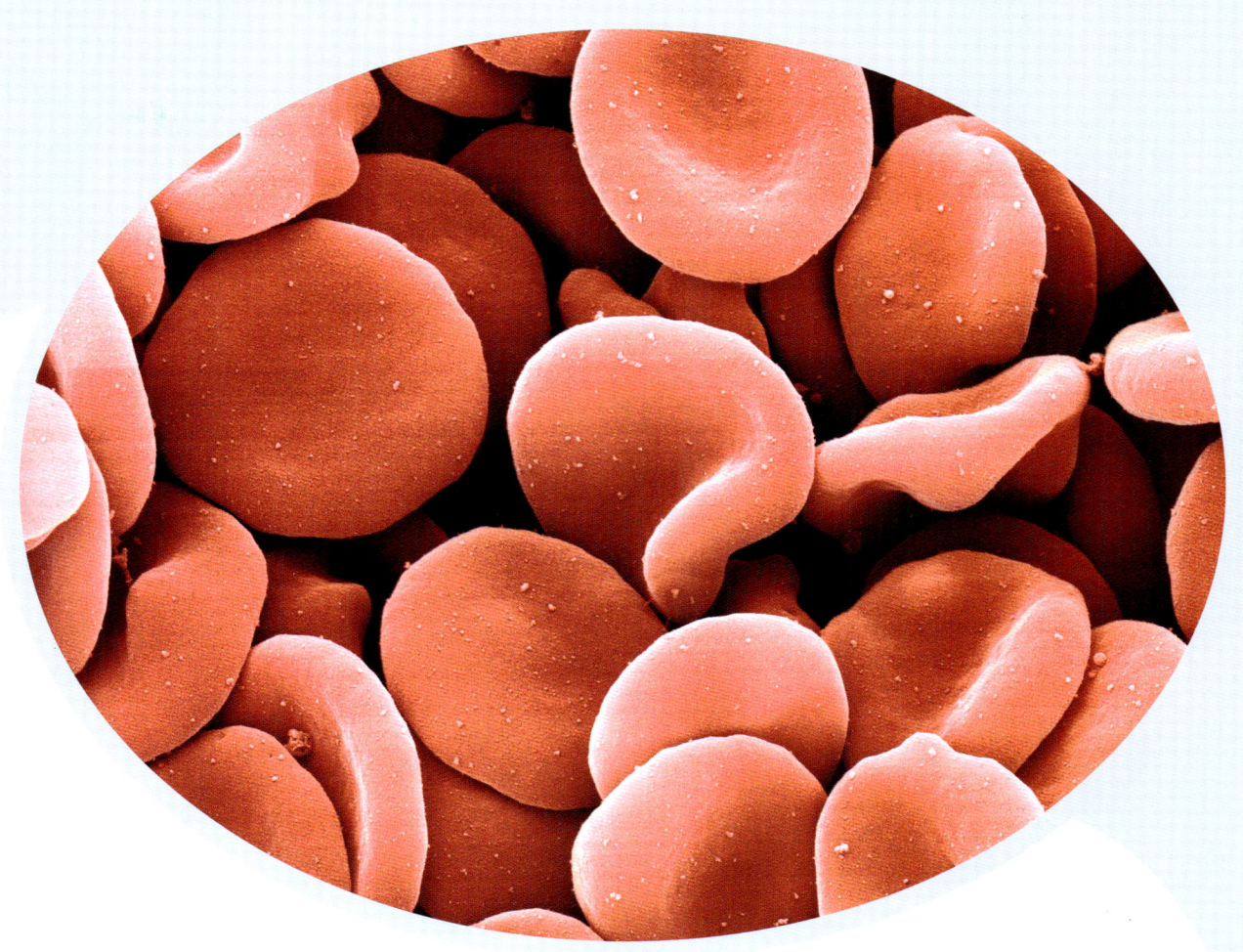

Human blood looks red because it contains red cells which carry **oxygen** around the body. But just as important are the white blood cells. These are larger and help the body to fight **disease**.

A tiny drop of blood contains millions of cells floating in liquid. Blood is pumped around the body so that the cells can do their work.

changing shape

Most young animals look like their parents, with the same basic body shape. But some go through different stages in a process called **metamorphosis**, which means "changing shape."

The eggs of frogs and toads first turn into **tadpoles**, which have simple bodies and tails. Tadpoles live and breathe under water.

The tadpole grows legs, loses its tail, and turns into a frog. The adult frog breathes air and can live out of water.

16

Many insects go through several stages. Their eggs first develop into **grubs**, like this caterpillar. The caterpillar will eventually turn into a **chrysalis**, which is a resting stage before it becomes an adult.

An insect's chrysalis is like a case. The adult butterfly goes on developing inside the case. Finally, it comes out and can stretch its beautiful wings before going on its first flight.

17

Chemical messengers

Our growth is controlled by special substances called **hormones**. These act as chemical messengers by carrying instructions from one set of cells to another.

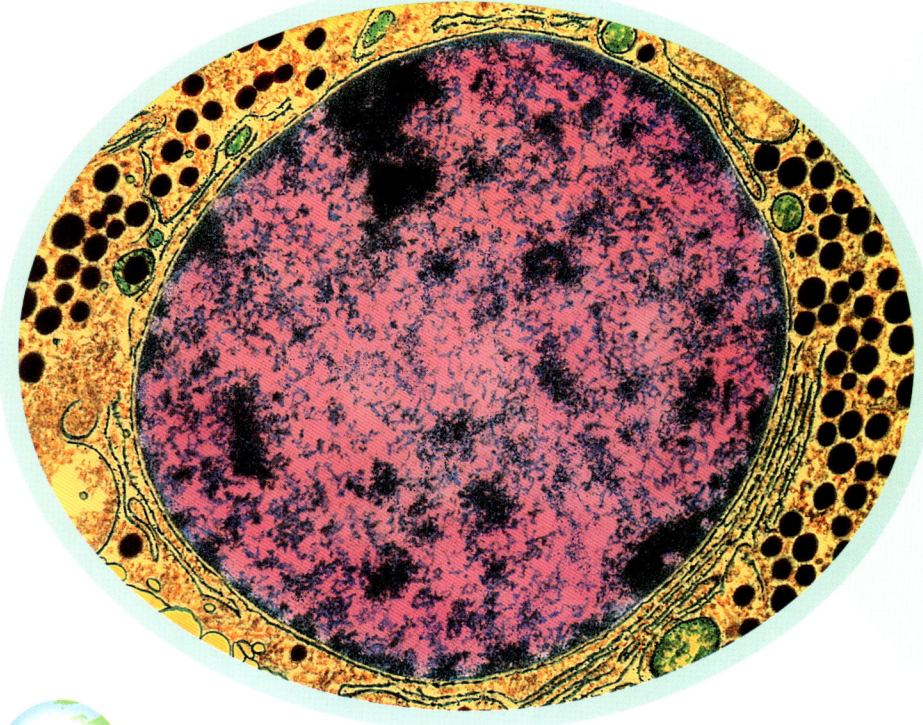

This magnified photograph shows the special chemical messenger called growth hormone. This is very important when we are young and growing.

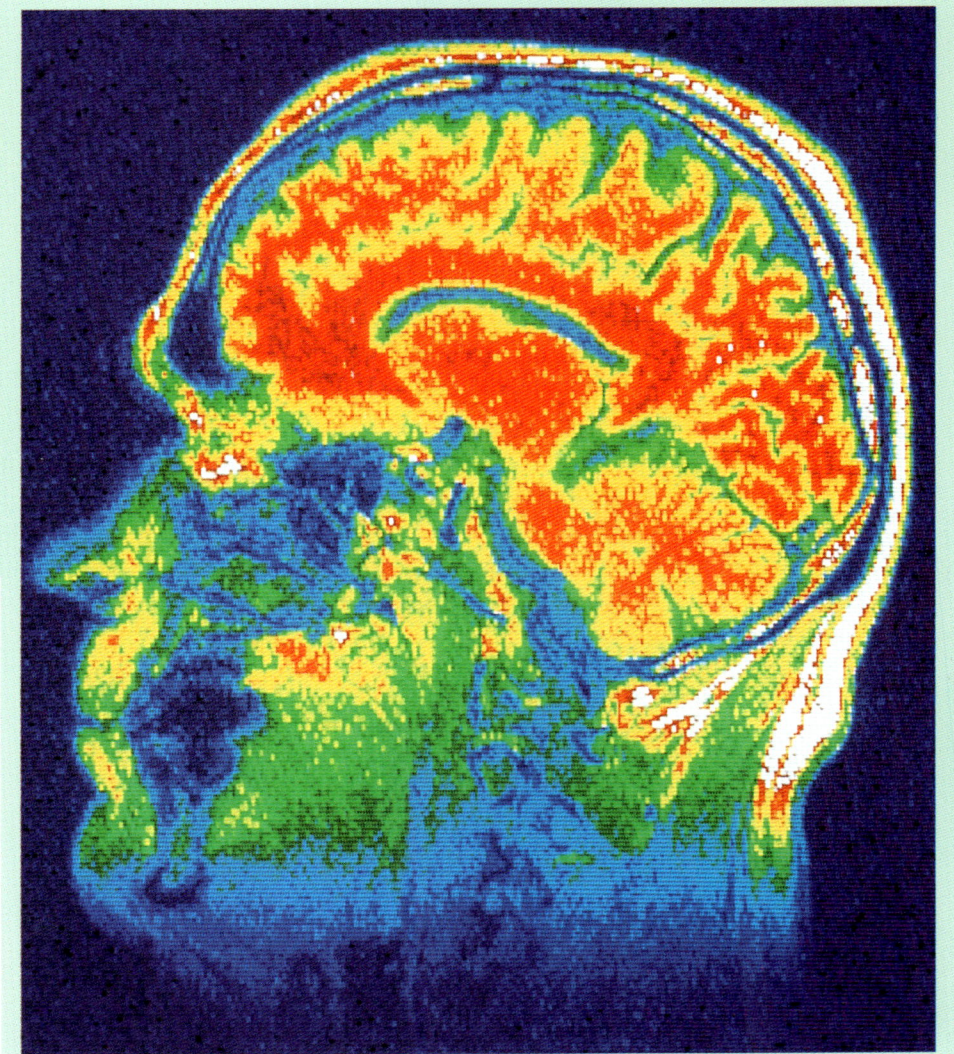

All the body's messages and movements are controlled by the brain. It is well protected by our **skull**.

Hormones carry their messages by traveling throughout our bodies in our blood. A **gland** near the center of the head produces a special growth hormone, which controls the growth of bones and muscles.

Growing and learning

As young animals develop, it is not only their bodies that change and grow. Their **behavior** also changes, as they learn more and more about the world around them.

Like these bear cubs, many young animals stay close to their parents and learn from them.

Young children love to play with blocks and other toys. At the same time, they learn about shapes and sizes. If the tower isn't straight, it will fall.

Young mammals, including humans, learn a lot through play. Many young animals play at fighting as they learn to hunt and defend themselves. Young children enjoy playing with toys and learn a lot at the same time.

How plants grow

Plants grow from seeds. A seed from inside this almond nut has taken root and started to grow.

Plants make their own food by capturing the sun's energy in their leaves. They also take in gas from the air and water from the soil. All this makes a form of sugar, which is sent around the plant.

As the roots of this pea plant grow down into the soil, its stem starts to grow up toward the light.

Most plants carry on growing throughout their lives. A plant's leaves, flowers, and fruits usually grow to a fixed size, but its **roots** and **stem** may continue to grow until the plant finally dies.

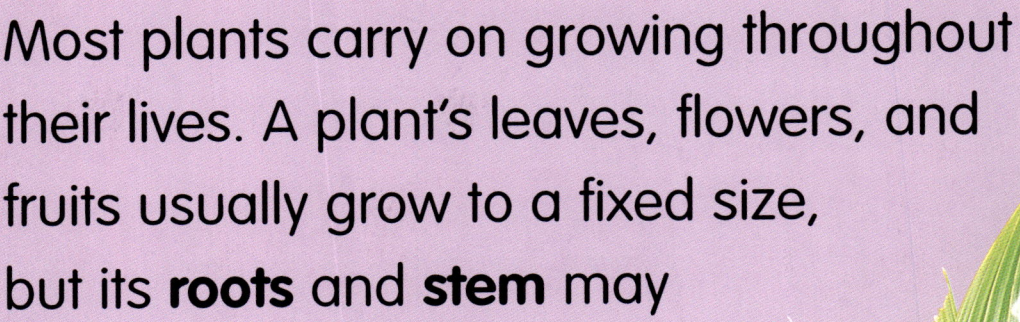

A plant's leaves grow out from the stem, ready to catch the sunlight. When it is fully grown, this coconut palm will produce seeds to make more young plants in the future.

The growing season

Plants cannot move around like animals, so they are much more dependent on their surroundings. These often change a lot with the different seasons.

This oak tree is covered in leaves during the summer. This means that it can make lots of food, and grow and produce seeds.

Most plants have a growing season, usually the hot summer. Some plants, called **annuals**, put all their energy into growth in a single season. They develop from a seed, then flower and produce their own seeds all in one year, before dying.

The oak tree has now shed its leaves for winter, when there is less sunlight. It does this to save energy and water, and spends the winter as if asleep.

Life cycle

Growth is an important part of every living thing's **life cycle**, which begins when its first cell is formed. Most animals continue growing until they are adults, when they are able to **reproduce** and have children.

This bristlecone pine tree is very old. Some of these trees have lived for thousands of years.

Once they become adult insects, mayflies live for just a few days.

The life cycle of some insects may last only a few weeks. Most larger animals have longer lives, though few live as long as human beings. The cycle ends when an individual animal or plant dies.

Exercise helps our muscles and bones grow strong and healthy. It can also help us to live longer.

Do it yourself

These two fun activities show how plants grow.

Growing beans

1 Cut blotting paper to fit around the insides of two empty jam jars, and put crumpled paper towels in the jars. Place bean seeds between the blotting paper and the sides of the jars.

2 Then turn one jar on its side. Keep the jars in a warm place out of direct sunlight, water the paper towels regularly, and watch shoots and roots appear. See how the shoots head for the light.

Growing sunflowers

1 Grow a few sunflower seeds in separate pots and keep them indoors until they are about 2 inches tall.

2 Then plant the seedlings outside in a sunny patch of soil. Tie them to a cane as they grow. You could keep a weekly record of each sunflower's height.

Glossary

annuals Plants that live for only one year.

behavior The way in which a living thing acts.

cell The smallest unit of a living thing, so tiny that it can be seen only through a microscope.

chrysalis The stage of an insect, especially a butterfly or moth, before it becomes an adult.

disease Illness.

divides Splits into parts.

energy The strength needed to do things.

food chain A series of living things in which each is dependent on the next one down for food.

gland An organ in the body that produces hormones and other important substances.

grubs The young stage of some insects. Small grubs are also called maggots; larger grubs are caterpillars.

hormones Important substances in living things which carry chemical messages.

life cycle The series of changes in the life of a living thing.

metamorphosis The process of changing into an adult in different stages.

multiplying Increasing in number.

oxygen A gas in the air which humans and animals need to breathe in order to live.

proteins Important substances in living things which help them to grow and be strong and healthy.

reproduce To produce young.

roots Parts of a plant that grow down into soil.

skull The framework of bones that protects the brain.

stem The main stalk of a plant.

tadpoles The young of frogs or toads with tails and no legs.

teenagers Young people between the ages of 13 and 19.

index

animals 4, 10, 13, 14, 16, 20, 24, 26, 27

birds 5, 13

blood 15, 19

bones 9, 10, 14, 19, 27

brain 19

cells 4, 5, 6, 14, 15, 18, 26, 30

children 7, 8, 11, 21, 26

eggs 4, 5, 16, 17

elephants 11, 13

energy 8, 12, 22, 25, 30

food 12, 13, 22, 24

food chain 13, 30

frogs 4, 16

growing 4, 5, 6, 7, 8, 9, 10, 11, 12, 14, 16, 18, 19, 20, 22, 23, 24, 25, 27, 28, 29

hormones 18, 30

human babies 6, 7, 12, 20

insects 13, 17, 26, 27

learning 7, 20, 21

lions 13

meat eaters 13

muscles 9, 11, 19, 27

plant eaters 12, 13

plants 22, 23, 24, 25, 28, 29

proteins 12, 30

seeds 22, 23, 24, 25, 28, 29

sheep 12